D1552097

Table of Contents

Introduction

Stories are provided at a variety of levels ranging from simple words that name pictures for prereaders to more complex text for emerging readers. All of the stories include a picture Story Dictionary and illustrations that enhance the text.

Reproduce the stories in this book and prepare story booklets for individual students.

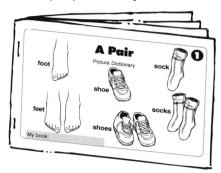

Before giving a new reading story to a student or group of students, take time to develop a context of experiences that will help your readers to succeed.

You may:
- read the stories together,
- have small groups of students read the stories,
- have partners read a story together, or
- have individuals read the stories independently.

Use the skill pages following the stories:
- to assess students' comprehension,
- to reinforce emergent reading skills,
- to reinforce phonics instruction, and
- to provide opportunities for students to develop and practice oral and written language.

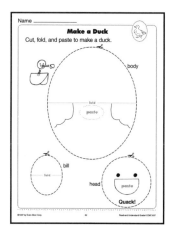

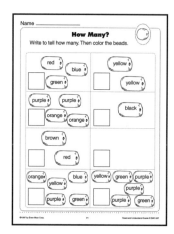

Steps to Follow

1. Prereading experiences

Concrete experiences that help to develop vocabulary about the subject of a story are important to the success of reading the story. For example:

- Draw attention to your dismissal time practices before reading *Time to Go.*
- Pattern with colored beads before reading **Read the Beads.**
- Eat a snack on the playground and fly a kite before reading **In the Sky**.

Ask questions to help students make connections to their own experiences.

- Before reading **The Pet Store**, you might ask "Have you ever visited a pet store?" "What animals did you see?" "Where were the animals kept?"

2. Preview the story with your students

- Look first at the words presented in the Story Dictionary.
  "Who can use the Story Dictionary to read the new words from the story?"

- Then page through the story together. Have the readers look at the illustrations and predict what they think is happening on the pages. Listen closely to the vocabulary used. Suggest words or phrases that are used in the story vocabulary that seem to be unfamiliar to the readers. "What kinds of things do kittens do? They run, jump, pounce, scratch, play, and meow."

- You may want to write words as you talk about them or ask the readers to locate the words on a specific page.
  "Can you find the word *Meow* on this page?"

3. Read

4. Completing skill pages

- Before expecting students to complete the skill pages independently, model appropriate responses with your students.

- Some of the phrases in the directions on the skill pages will need to be read with students.

- When students draw in a response to a question, provide an opportunity for the students to describe and explain their drawing. If possible, write what they say beside their pictures.

Time to Go

Picture Dictionary

coat

dad

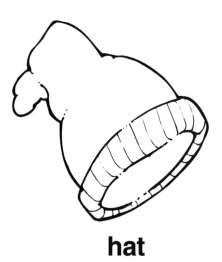

hat

My book:

2

my coat

©1997 by Evan-Moor Corp.

3

my hat

4

my dad

Time to go.

EMC 637

Name _____

Remembering the Story

Draw a line to show what happened.

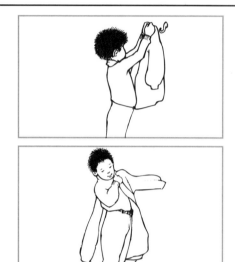

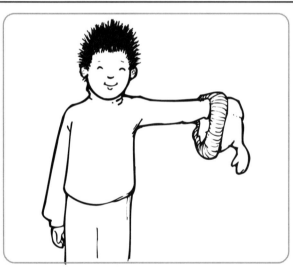

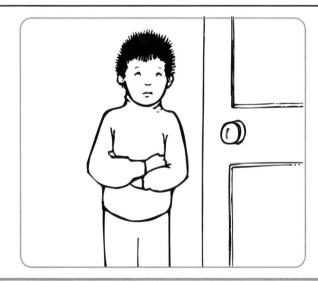

Name _____

Hang Them Up

Hang up the coat.

Hang up the hat.

paste

paste

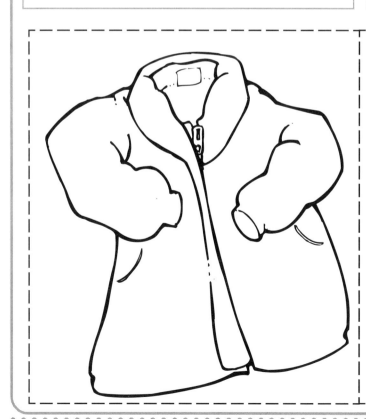

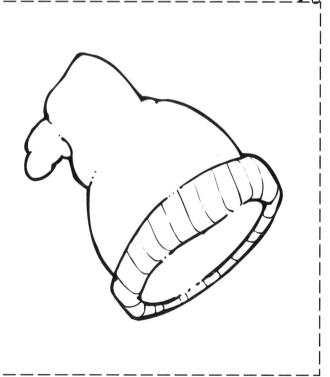

Name _____

Going Home

Draw a line to show the boy how to get home.

Read and Understand Grade K EMC 637

Name _____

Same Sound

Color the pictures that begin with the same
sound as  .
dad

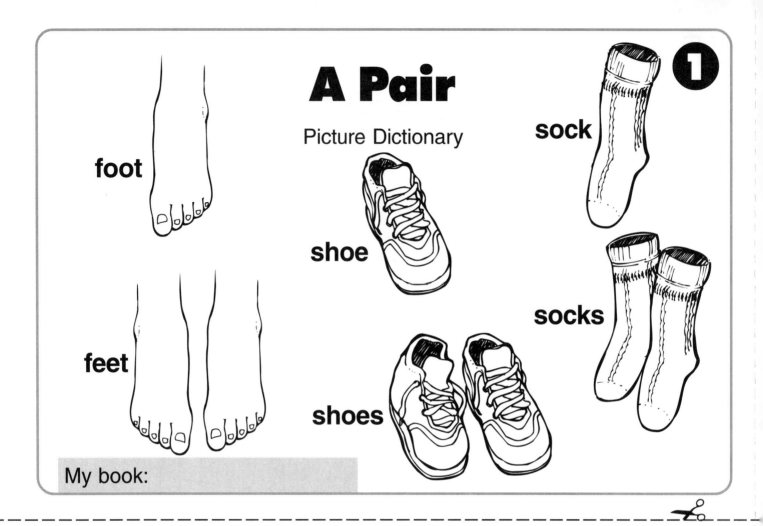

A Pair

Picture Dictionary

foot

feet

shoe

shoes

sock

socks

My book:

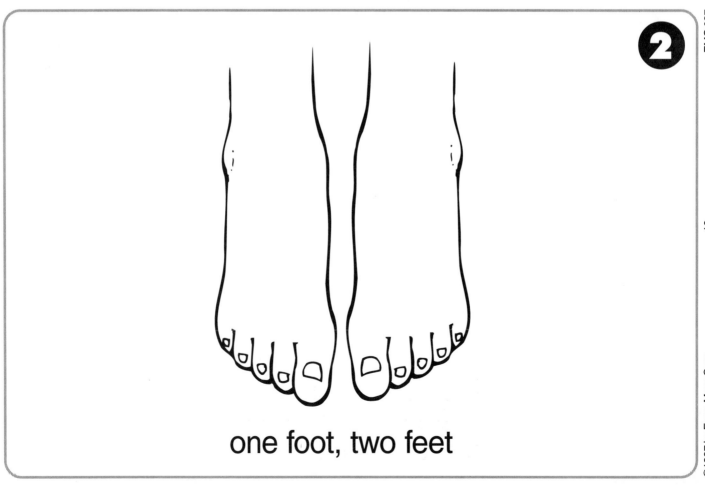

one foot, two feet

EMC 637

one sock, two socks

✂

one shoe, two shoes

EMC 637

Remembering the Story

Cut and paste to show what happened.

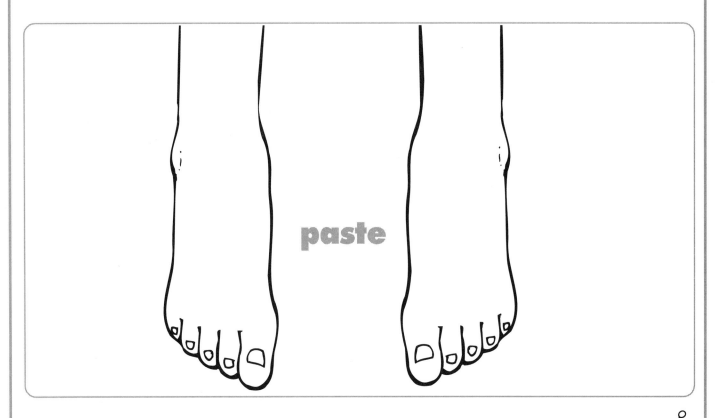

paste

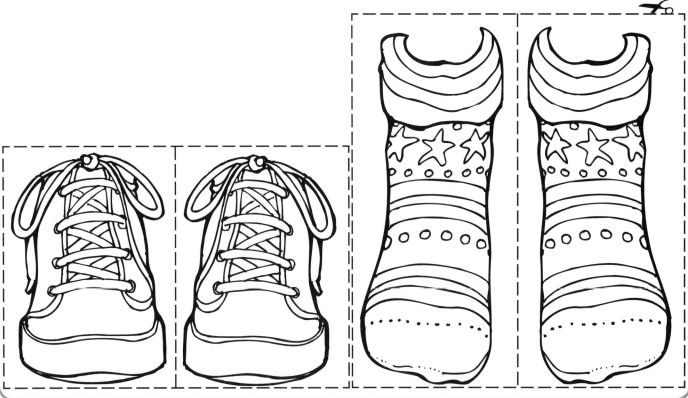

How Many?

Write the number to show how many.

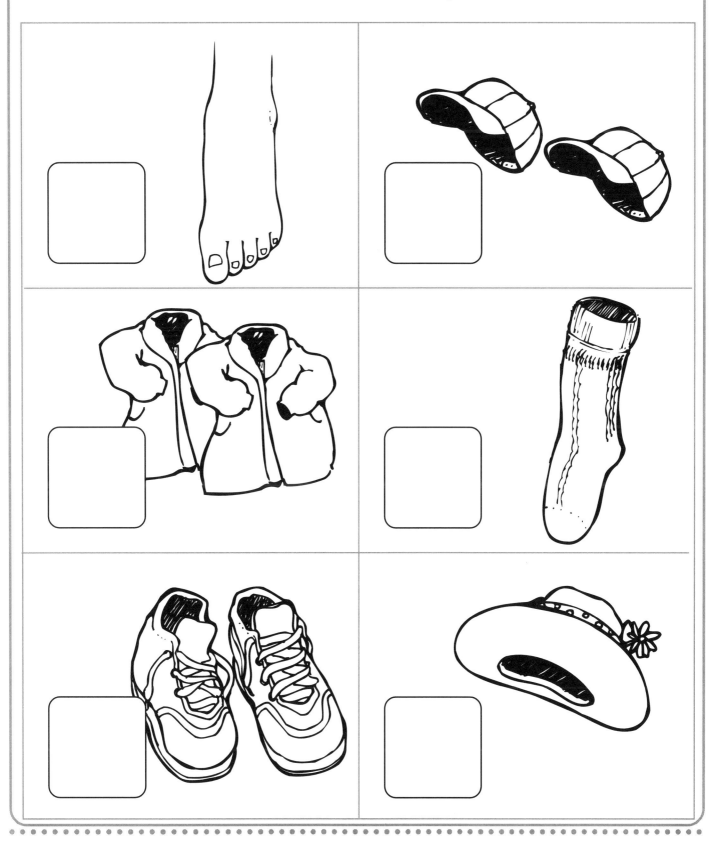

Name _____

Circle the pictures that begin with the same sound as 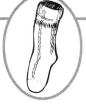 .

 sock

How many did you find? ⬜

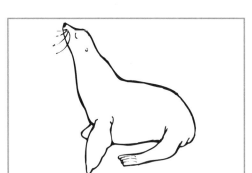

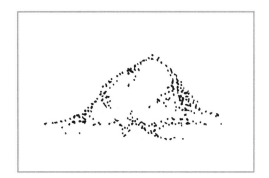

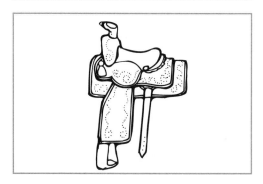

Whose Shoes?

Draw a line to show whose shoes.

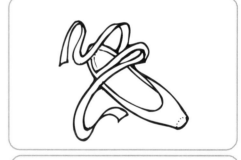

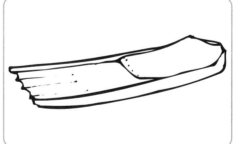

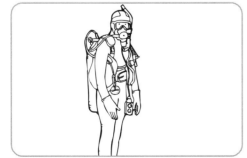

The Pet Store

Picture Dictionary

cat

dog

Gila monster

My book:

EMC 637

Hi, dog.

Hi, cat.

EMC 637

Bye, Gila monster!

Name _____

Remembering the Story

Circle the picture that answers the question.

What animals did the girl see?

What animals did the girl like?

What animal scared the girl?

What animal would you like to buy?

18   Read and Understand Grade K EMC 637

Name _____

Where Do the Animals Belong?

Cut and paste.

paste	paste
	paste

✂

fold —————————

fold —————————

fold —————————

Name _____

Same Sound

Cut and paste to show what pictures begin with the same sound as 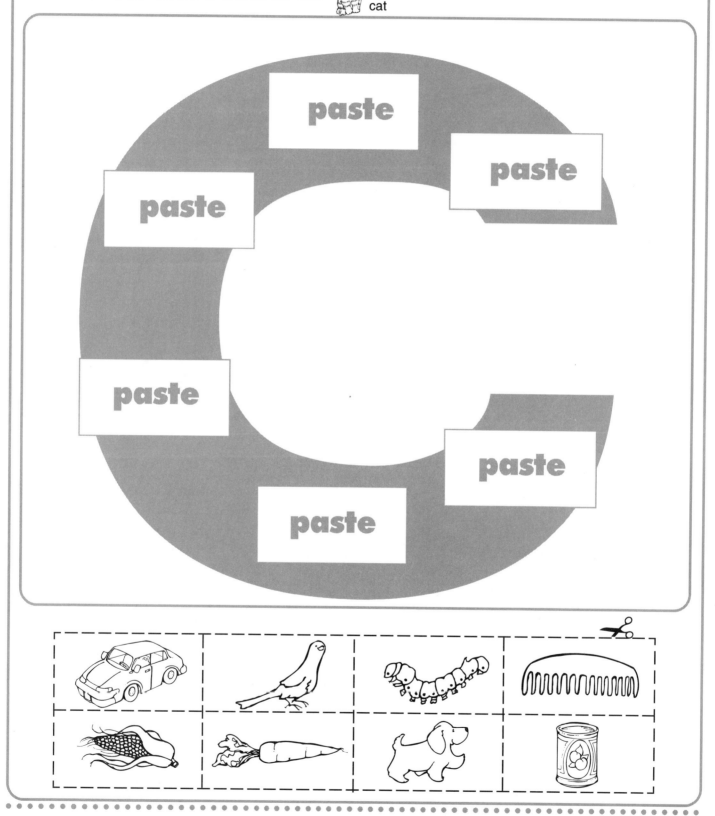 cat.

paste

paste

paste

paste

paste

paste

©1997 by Evan-Moor Corp.

Read and Understand Grade K EMC 637

Color the Cat

red

white

yellow

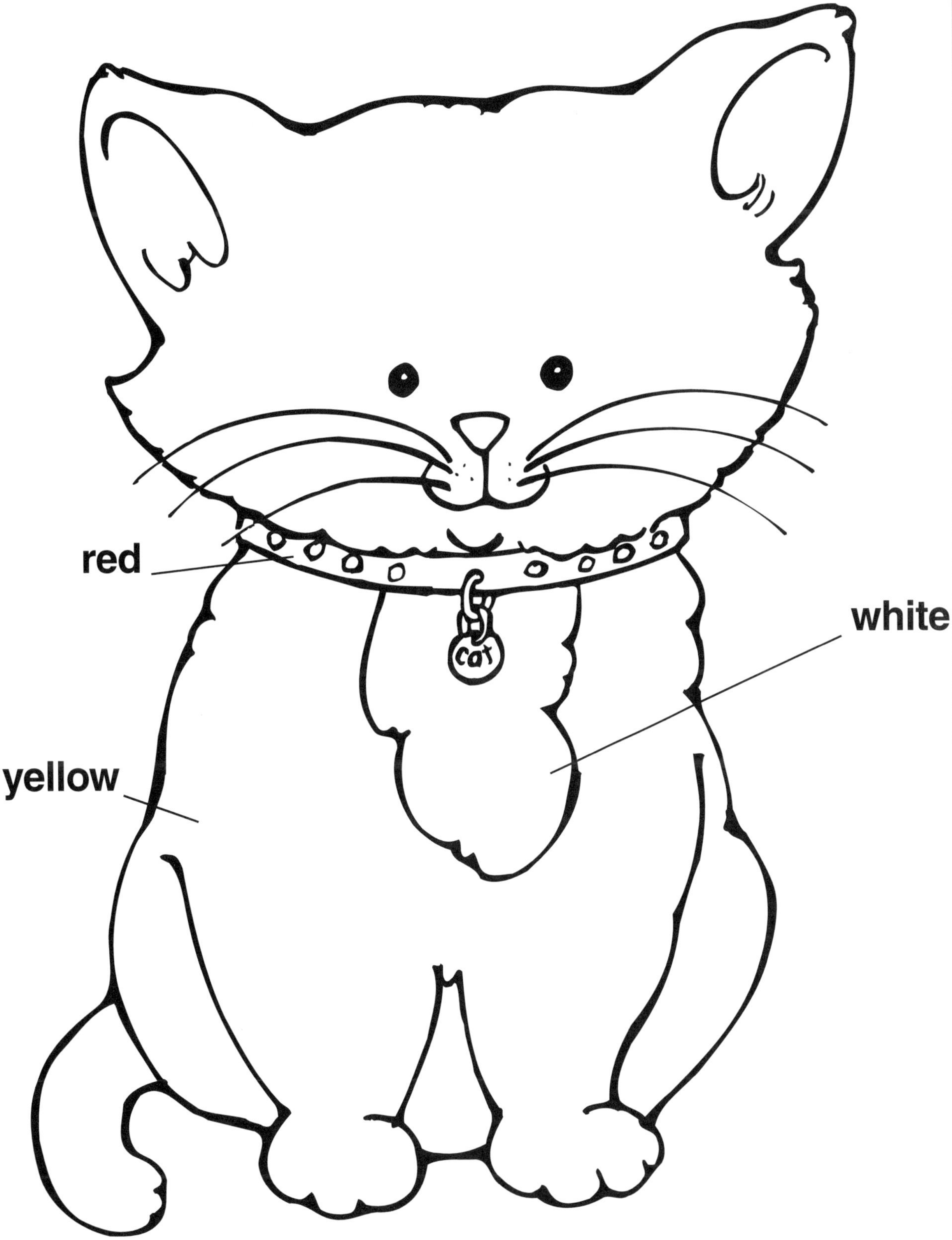

Picture Dictionary

up

ground

down

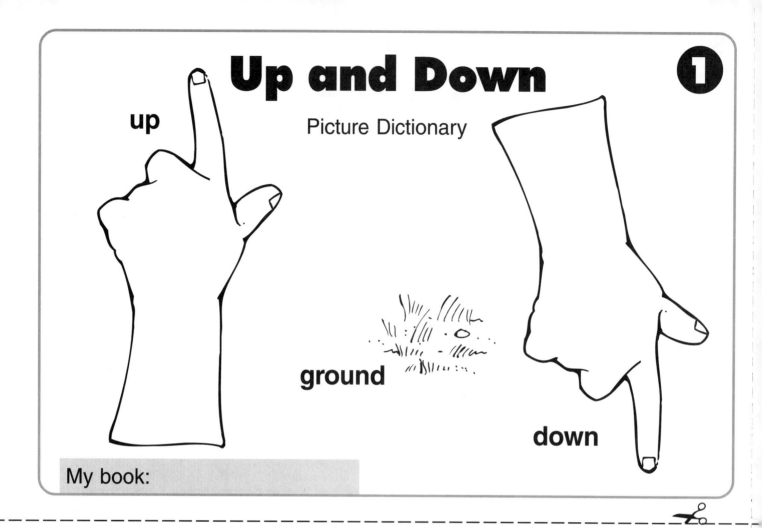

My book:

2

EMC 637

We are up.

We are down.

EMC 637

We are on the ground.

Name _____

Remembering the Story

Cut and paste to show up and down.

Up	Down	Up	Down
paste	paste	paste	paste

Read and Understand Grade K EMC 637

Up or Down

Circle up or down.

up   down

up   down

up   down

up   down

Name _____

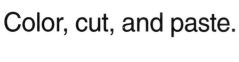

Match the Shape

Color, cut, and paste.

circle: paste

triangle: paste

square: paste

---✂

yellow

red

blue

Read and Understand Grade K EMC 637

Name _____

On the Playground

Draw to show yourself on the playground.

I am up.

I am down.

Read and Understand Grade K EMC 637

Where Does It Sleep? ①

Picture Dictionary

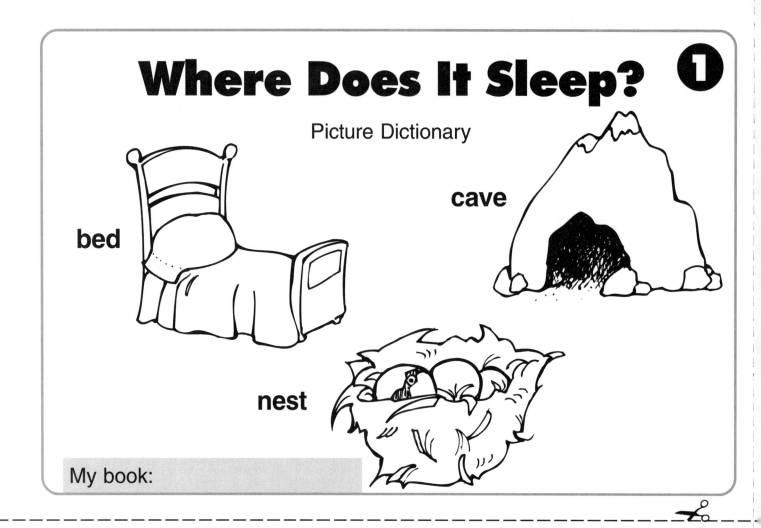

bed

cave

nest

My book:

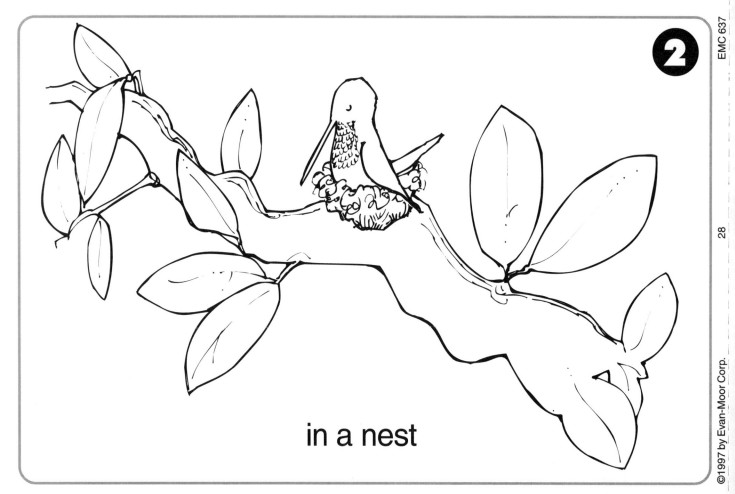

②

in a nest

EMC 637

in a cave

in a bed

EMC 637

Name _____

Remembering the Story

Draw a line to show where each sleeps.

 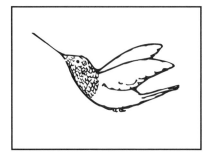 

  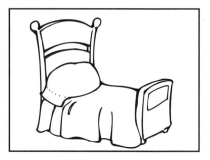

Draw to show where you sleep.

Name _____

Same Sound

Circle the pictures that begin with the same sound as .

boy

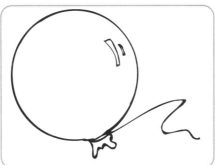

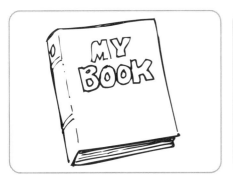

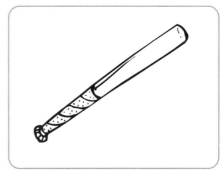

Read and Understand Grade K EMC 637

Name _____

Are You Awake?

Cut and paste to show awake and asleep.

Awake		**Asleep**	
paste	paste	paste	paste
paste	paste	paste	paste

Name _____

Following Directions

Draw a circle in the box.

Draw a triangle in the box.

Draw a face in the box.

Draw a square in the box.

Let's Go for a Ride

Picture Dictionary

car

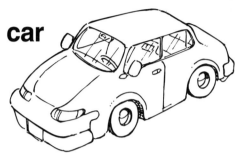

wagon

plane

My book:

We ride in a wagon.

EMC 637

We ride in a car.

EMC 637

We ride in a plane.

Name _____

Remembering the Story

Draw to show who went for a ride.

Draw to show what they rode in.

Name _____

Same Sound

Cut and paste to show the pictures that begin
with the same sound as  wagon .

paste

paste

paste   paste

Name _____

Reading Colors

Color the car red.

Color the wagon blue.

Color the plane green.

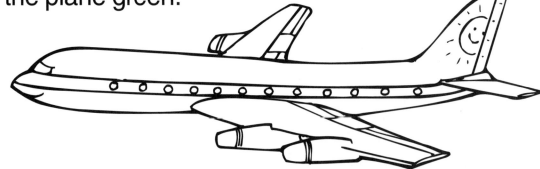

Name _____

I Can Ride

Circle the pictures to show the things that you can ride.

plane

lion

wagon

bike

dish

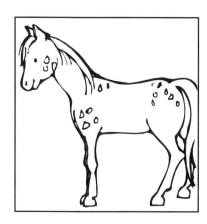

horse

hat

car

skateboard

Read and Understand Grade K EMC 637

Cars

Picture Dictionary

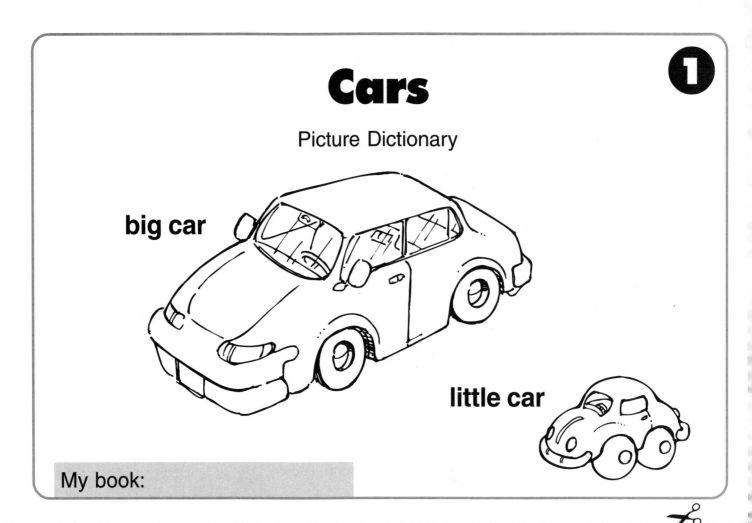

big car

little car

My book:

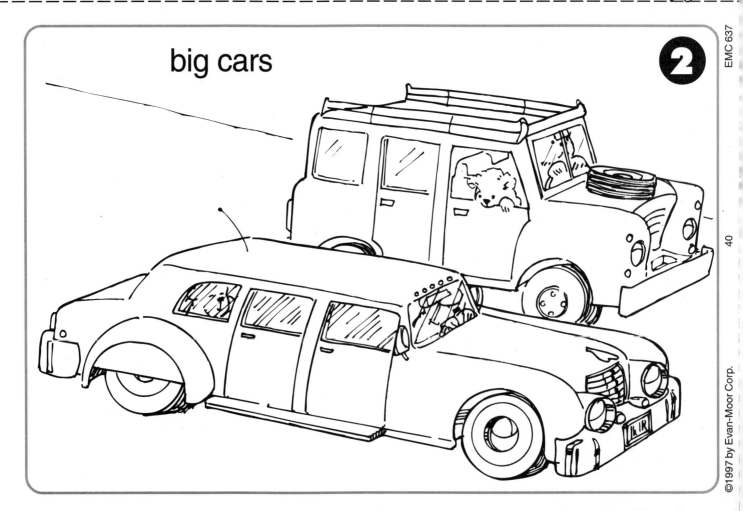

big cars

little cars

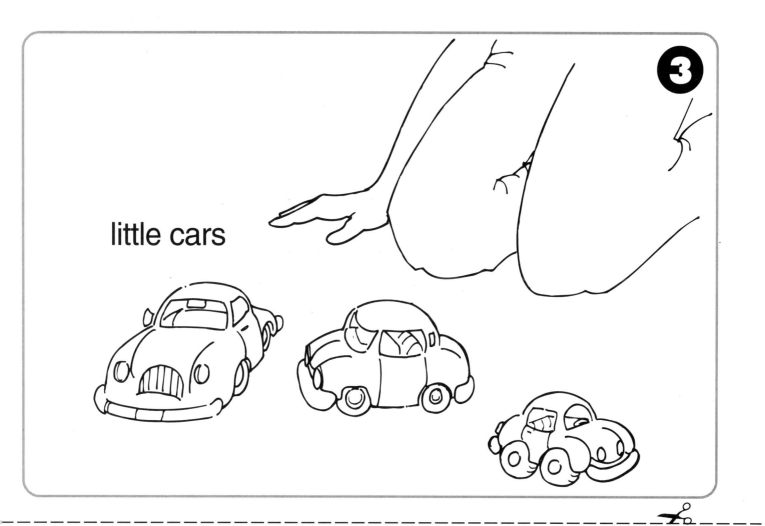

Look at all the cars.

EMC 637

Find the Car

Color the parts with a • to find the car.

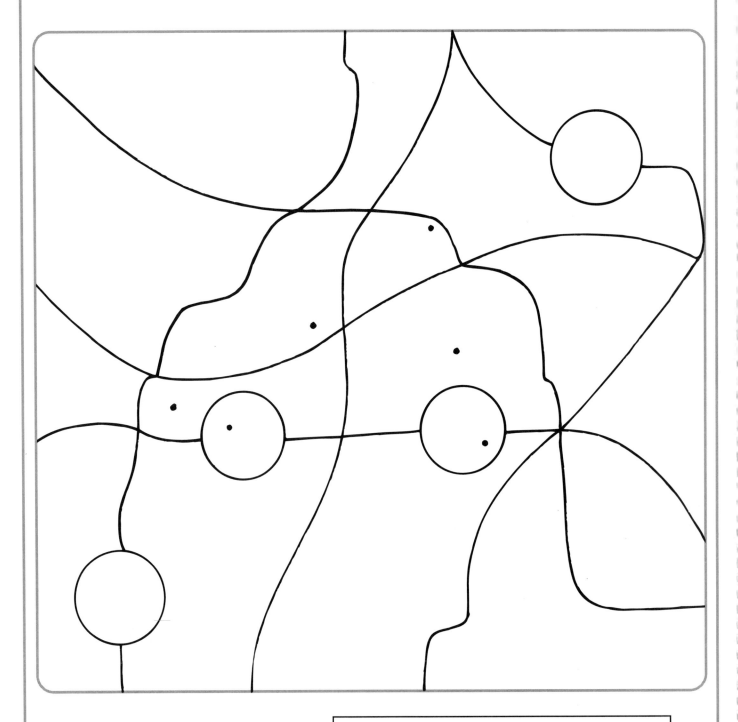

What color is your car? [   ]

Name _____

How Many?

Match the words and the pictures to tell how many.

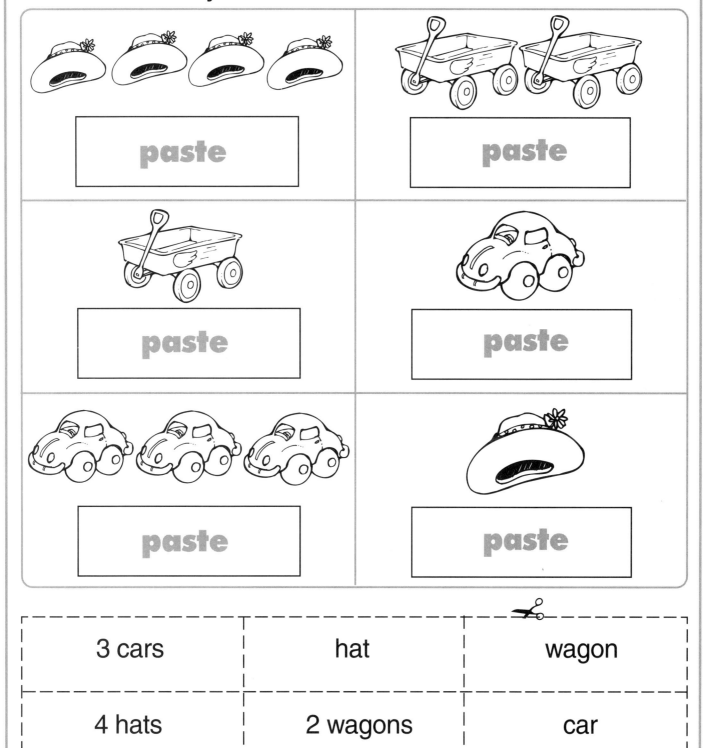

paste	paste
paste	paste
paste	paste

3 cars	hat	wagon
4 hats	2 wagons	car

Name _____

Big and Little

Draw four **big** things.

Draw four little things.

Tell about the big and little things.

Name _____

Same Sound

Cut and paste to show the pictures with the same beginning sound as  .

lion

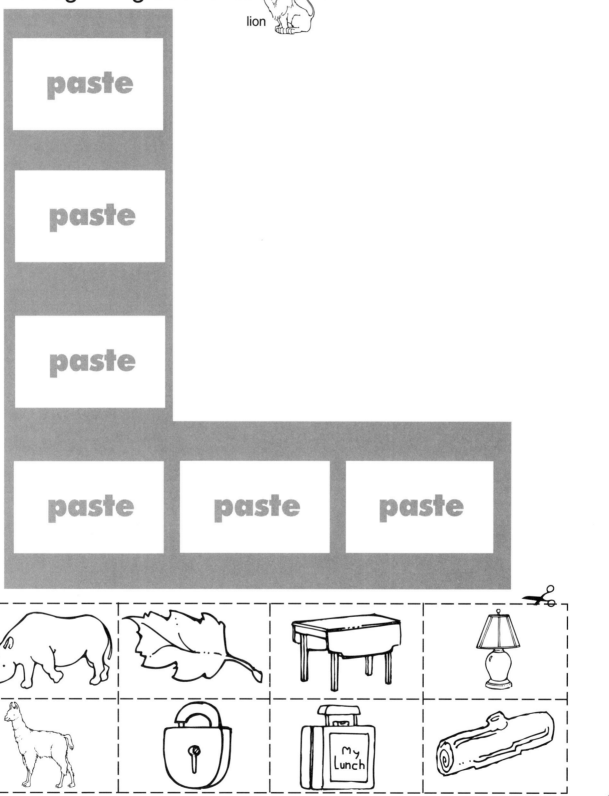

paste

paste

paste

paste   paste   paste

Which Hat?

Picture Dictionary

cowboy hat

stocking hat

hard hat

top hat

My book:

cowboy hat

hard hat

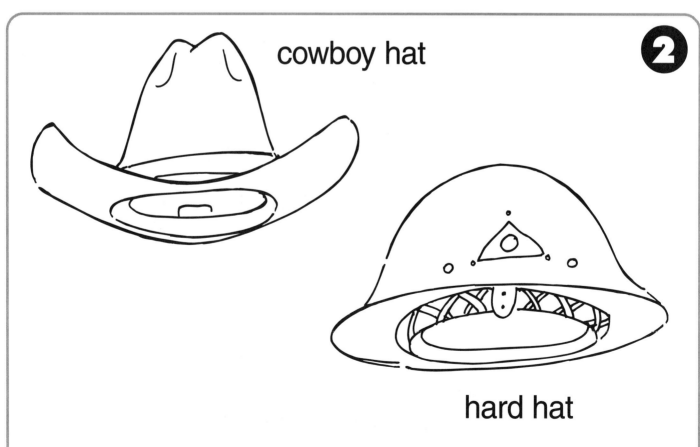

EMC 637

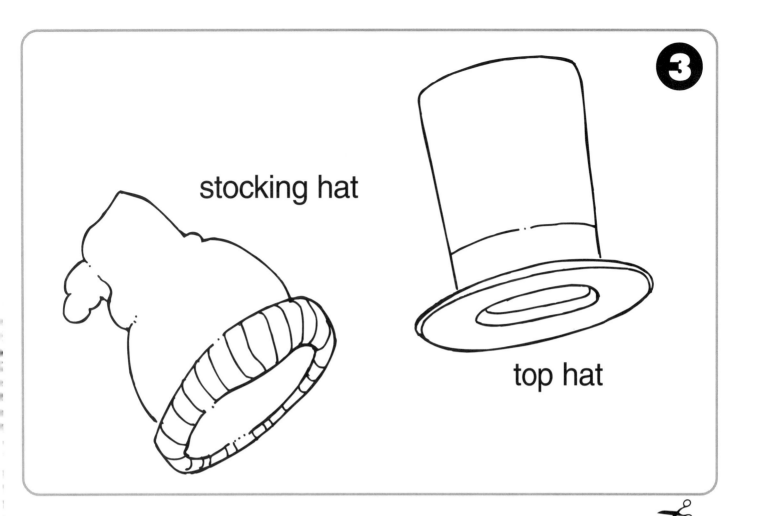

stocking hat

top hat

Which hat will you choose?

EMC 637

47

Name _____

Remembering the Story

Circle the hats in the story.

Draw to show which
hat you would choose.

Name _____

It Rhymes with Hat

Cut and paste to show the pictures that rhyme with 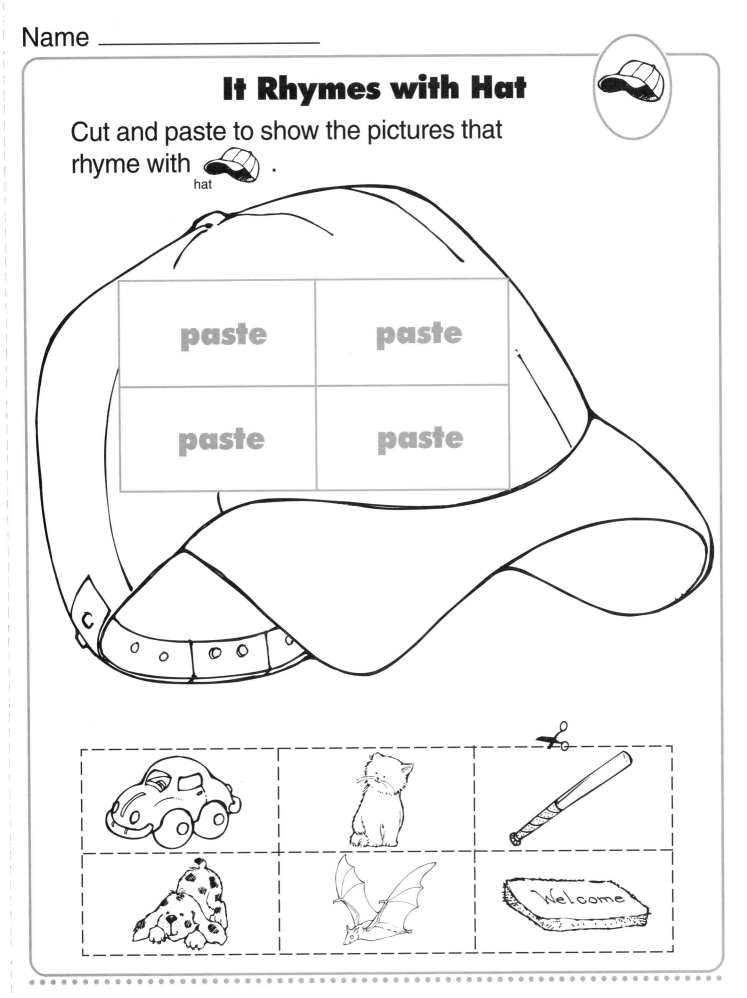 hat .

paste   paste

paste   paste

Whose Hat?

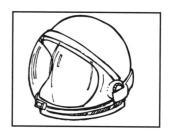

Draw a line to show whose hat.

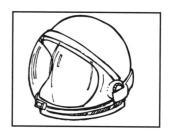

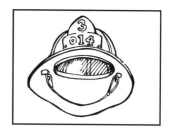

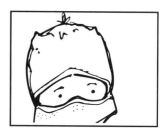

Read and Understand Grade K EMC 637

Name _____

Same Sound

Circle the pictures that begin with the same sound as .

hat

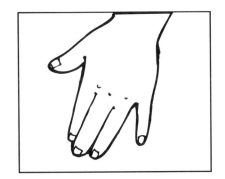

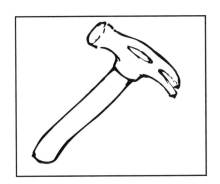

Read and Understand Grade K EMC 637

sun

In the Sky

Picture Dictionary

plane

kite

cloud

bird

rain

My book:

the sun, a bird, a plane

EMC 637

a kite, a cloud

and rain

EMC 637

Remembering the Story

Cut and paste. Put the pictures in order.
Tell the story.

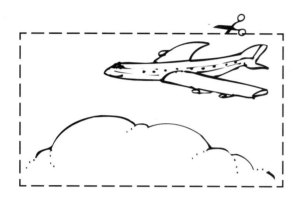

paste

paste

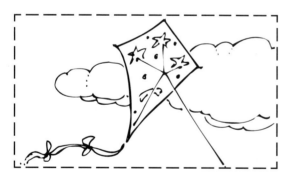

paste

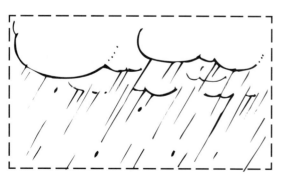

paste

Same Sound

Cut and paste to show what pictures begin
with the same sound as /////.

rain

What Can I Do?

Draw two things you would do on each day.

Sunny Day

Rainy Day

Name _____

What's in the Sky?

Connect the dots to see what's in the sky.
Start at 1.

Read and Understand Grade K EMC 637

Little Quackers

Picture Dictionary

1

quiet!

quack

My book:

2

Quack.

EMC 637

EMC 637

Remembering the Story

Cut and paste to tell what each character said.

Quack!

Quack,Quack, Quack.

Quiet!

Read and Understand Grade K EMC 637

Qu

**The letters qu stand for the sound you hear
at the beginning of quack and quiet.**

Cut and paste to finish this **Qu** quilt. Color all the pictures
that begin with the same sound as quack.

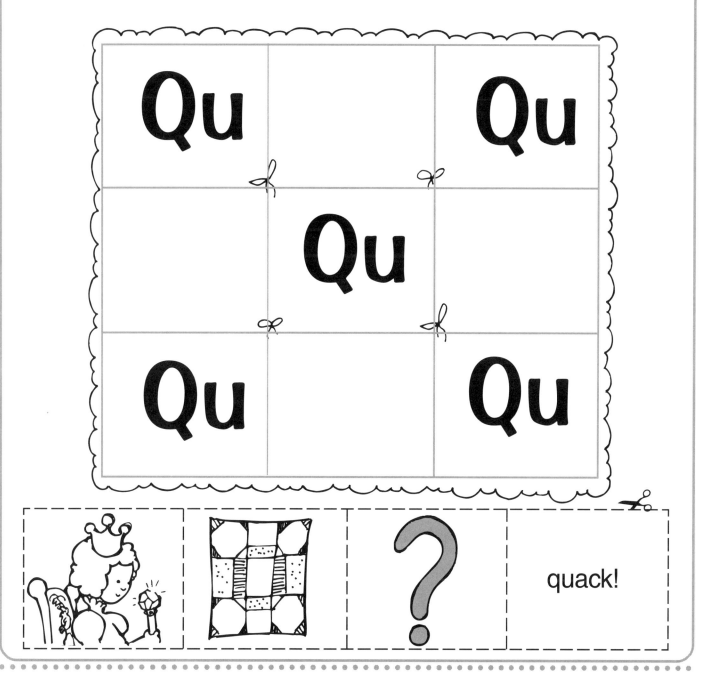

quack!

Make a Duck

Cut, fold, and paste to make a duck.

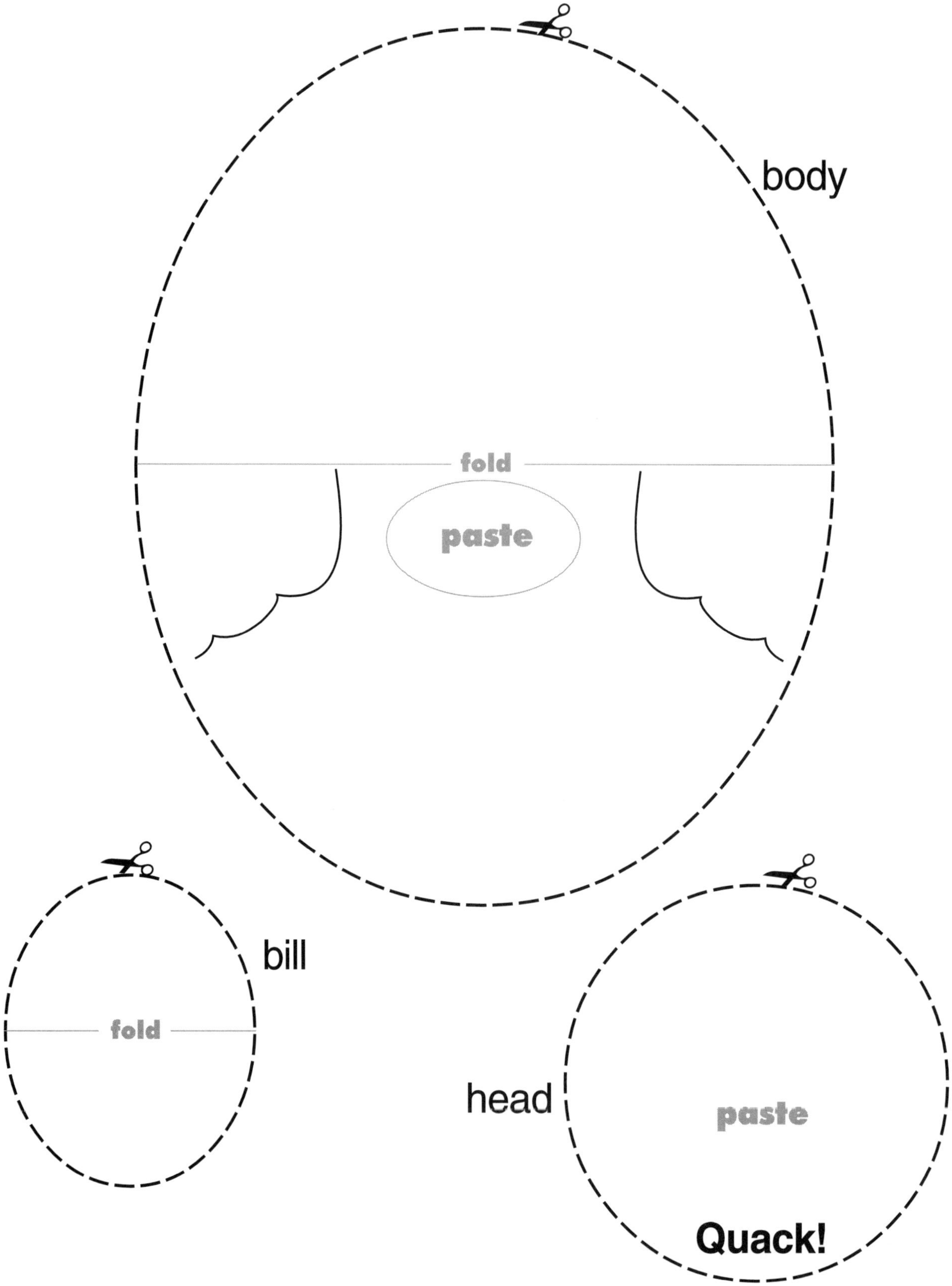

body

fold

paste

bill

fold

head

paste

Quack!

Noisy Animals

Draw to show what makes each sound.

Moooo	Quack
Woof-woof	Meow
Grrrrrrrr	Quiet!

Herbie

Picture Dictionary

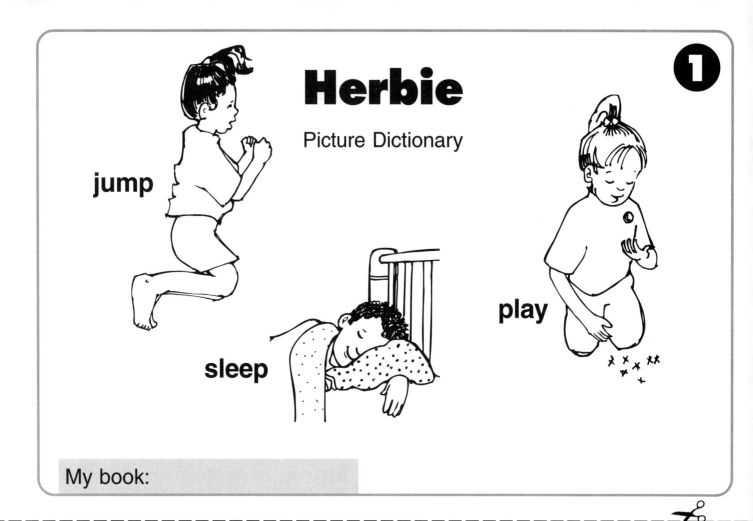

jump

sleep

play

My book:

EMC 637

Jump, Herbie, jump.
Meow!

Play, Herbie, play.
Meow!

EMC 637

Sleep, Herbie, sleep.
Purr!

Name _____

Remembering the Story

In this story...

Herbie is a

Herbie likes to

Herbie has a

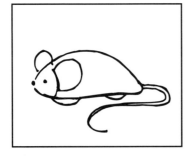 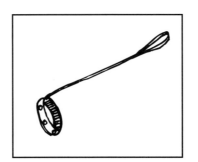 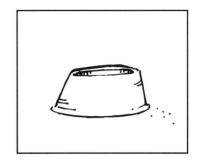

At the end, Herbie

took a walk   went to sleep   got a fish

Name _____

Same Sound

Cut and paste to show what pictures begin
with the same sound as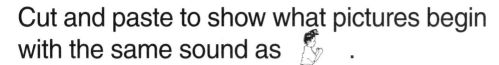

jump

paste	paste

paste

paste

paste

paste

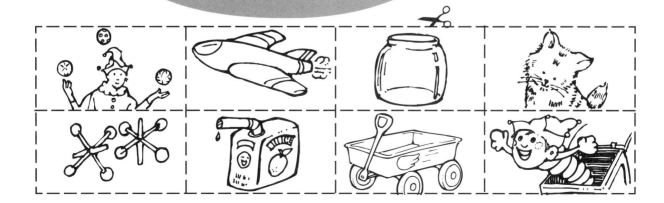

Name _____

Seeing Words

Circle the words that are the same as the first word in each row.

jump	jump　　run　　jump
play	pig　　play　　play
sleep	sleep　　slow　　sleep
meow	man　　mom　　meow
cat	car　　cat　　cat

Name _____

A New Page

Make a new page for your Herbie book.

- - - - - - - - - - - - - - - - - ✂ - - - - - - - - - -

_____, Herbie, _____

5

> Meow

- - - - - - - - - - - - - - - - - ✂ - - - - - - - - - -

Animal Babies

Picture Dictionary

bear

cat

dog

cow

horse

parent

My book:

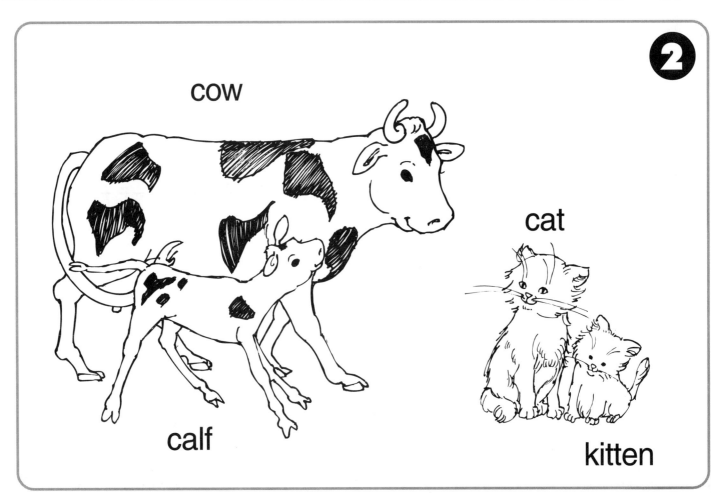

cow

cat

calf

kitten

EMC 637

horse

dog

pup

foal

EMC 637

parent

bear

child

cub

Remembering the Story

Cut and paste. Match the babies to their parents.

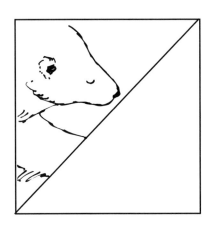

Name _____

Could It Be Real?

Circle yes or no to answer the question.

Could it be real?

yes   no

yes   no

yes   no

yes   no

yes   no

yes   no

Read and Understand Grade K EMC 637

Name _____

Growing Up

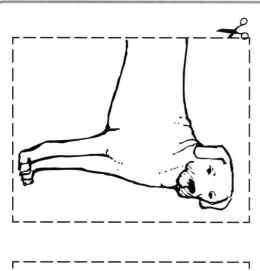

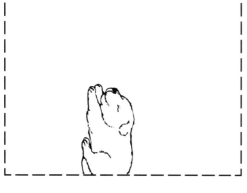

paste

paste

paste

paste

A Mini-Book

Draw pictures to make a mini-book.

My Animal Book

My Animal Book

by _____

bear

cat

cow

dog

horse

The Rainbow

Picture Dictionary

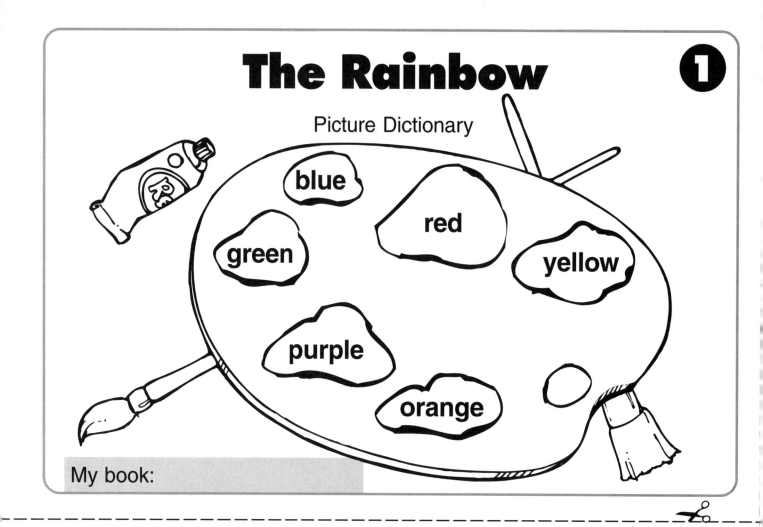

blue

red

green

yellow

purple

orange

My book:

EMC 637

Do you see the red?

Do you see the orange?

Do you see the yellow?

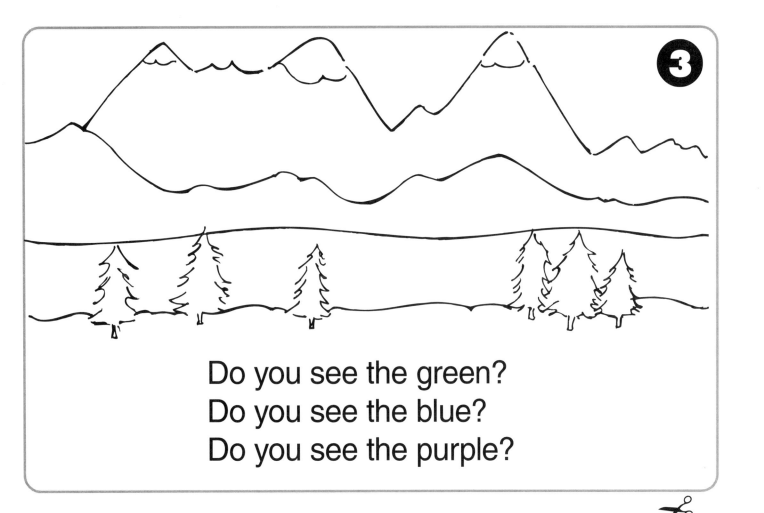

Do you see the green?
Do you see the blue?
Do you see the purple?

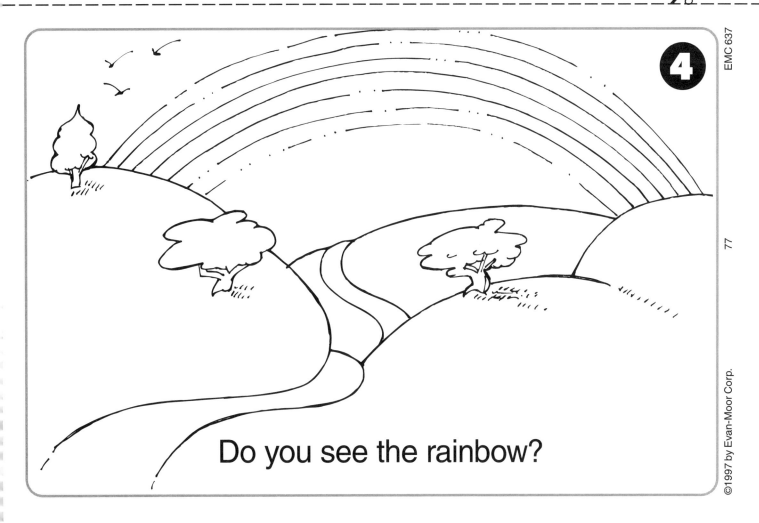

Do you see the rainbow?

EMC 637

Name _____

Read the Rainbow

Color the rainbow.

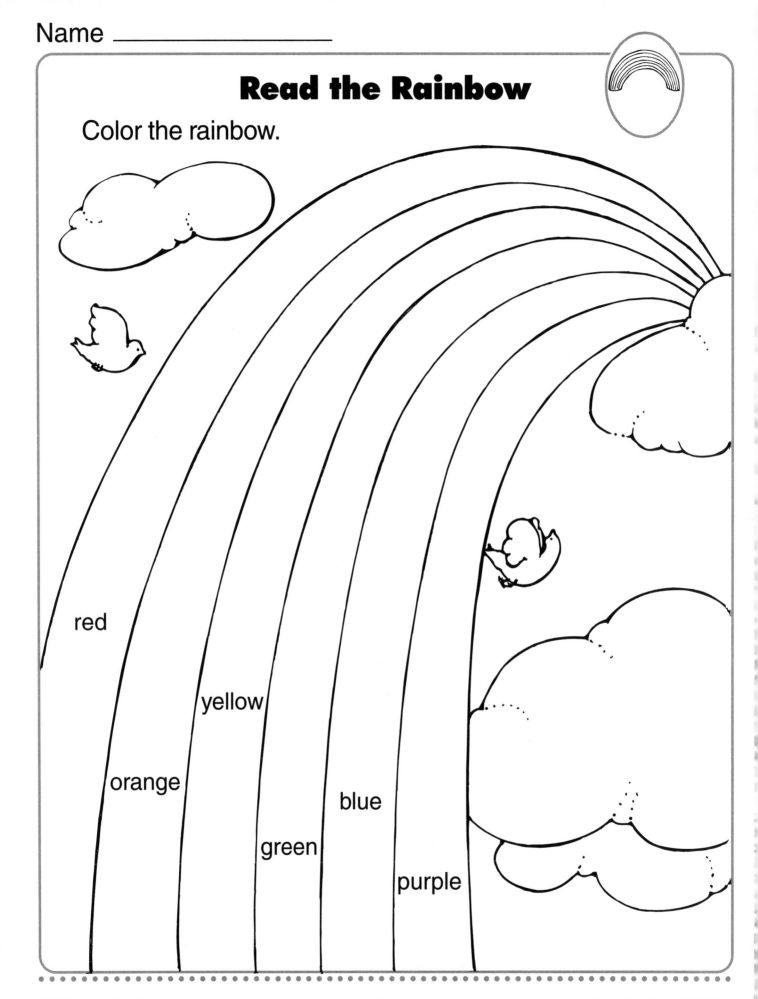

red

yellow

orange

blue

green

purple

78

Same Sound

Cut and paste to show the pictures that begin
with the same sound as yellow.

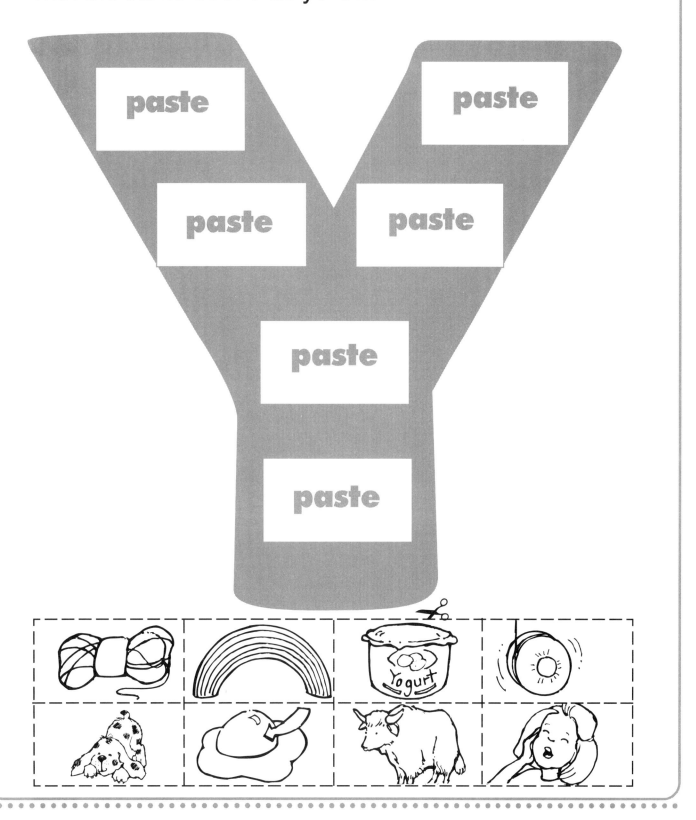

Name _____

Following Directions

Color the 🌷 red.   Color the 🍃 green.

Color the 🌺 orange.   Color the ✾ yellow.

Color the ✿ blue.   Color the 🦋 purple.

Read and Understand Grade K EMC 637

Name _____

How Many?

Write how many. Color the pictures.

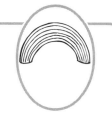

blue balls

yellow ducks

orange socks

purple car

green hats

red bugs

Read and Understand Grade K EMC 637

Can You?

Picture Dictionary

1

hop

run

jump

stop

My book:

2

I can run.
I can hop.

EMC 637

I can jump.
I can stop.

3

Can you run and hop?
Can you jump and stop?

4

EMC 637

Read the Words

?

Cut and paste to show what it says.

hop

jump

run

stop

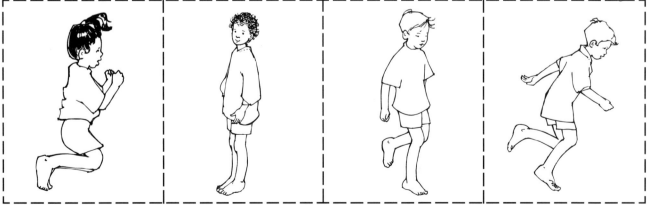

Name _____

All About You

Answer the questions.

Can you hop?   yes   no

Can you jump?   yes   no

Can you run?   yes   no

Can you stop?   yes   no

Draw to show something you can do.

Read and Understand Grade K EMC 637

Name _____

Words That Rhyme

Circle the words that rhyme.

1.

hop   drop   shop

2.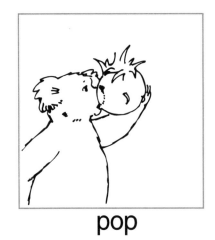

stop   mop   jump

3.

top   pop   run

What Is It?

?

Connect the dots to see what it is. Start with 1.
Then color the picture.

1 _____ 8

2

•7

3

•6

4

5

Read the Beads

Picture Dictionary

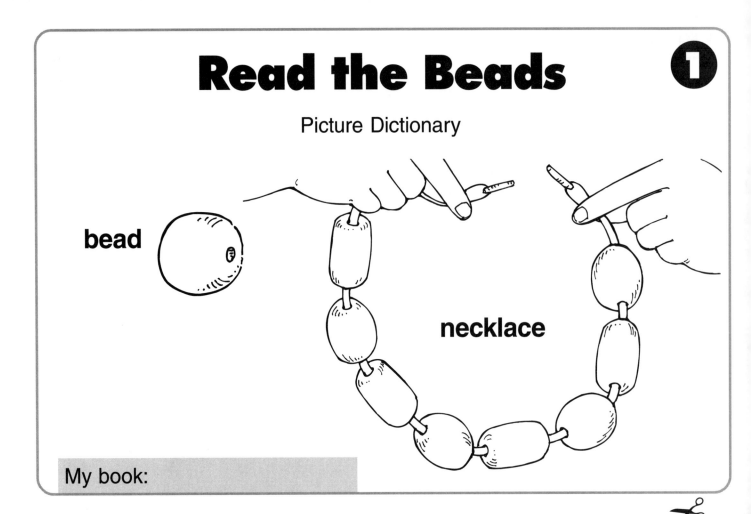

bead

necklace

My book:

EMC 637

one blue bead

one red bead

(Oh, a necklace.)

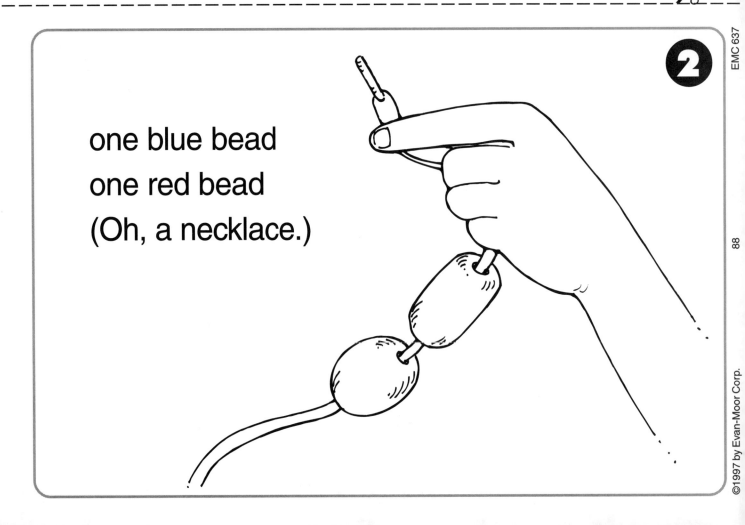

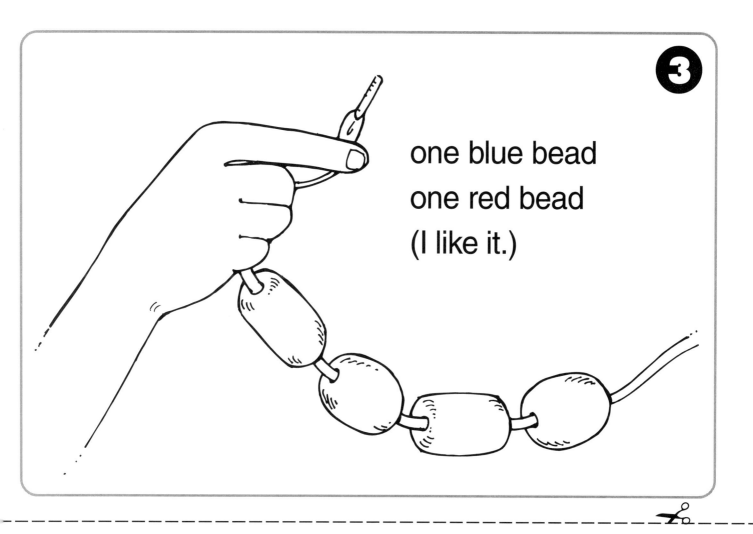

one blue bead

one red bead

(I like it.)

4

EMC 637

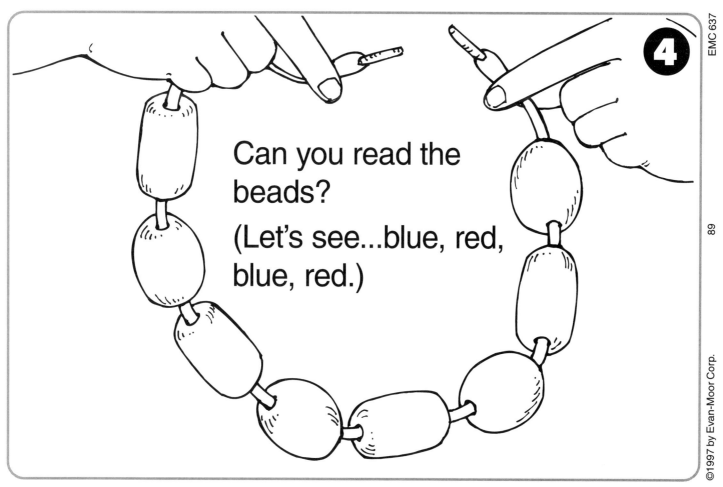

Can you read the beads?

(Let's see...blue, red, blue, red.)

Remembering the Story

Color, cut, and paste to make a necklace like the one in the story.

Name _____

How Many?

Write to tell how many. Then color the beads.

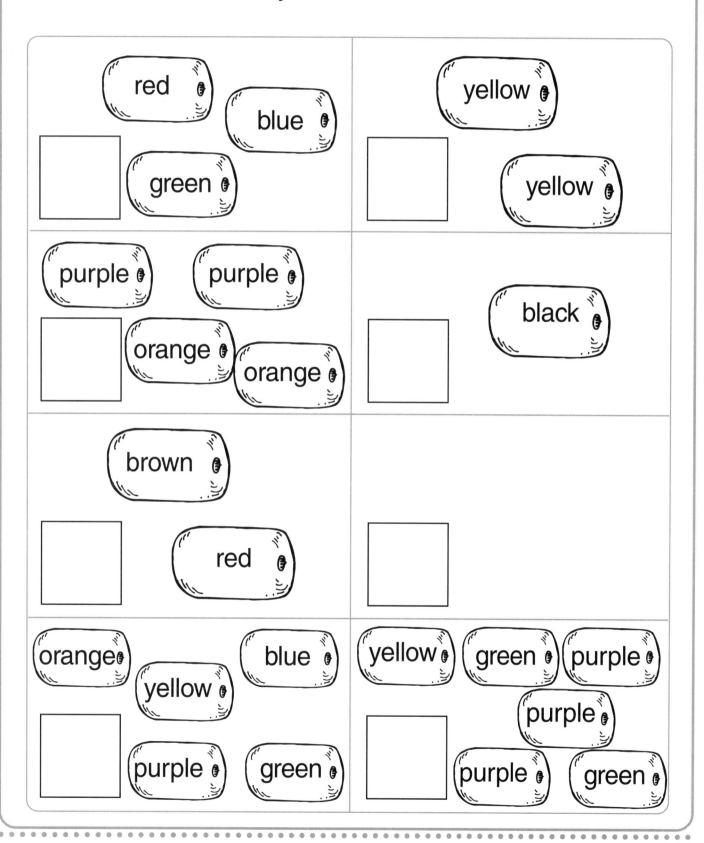

red   blue   green
[ ]

yellow   yellow
[ ]

purple   purple   orange   orange
[ ]

black
[ ]

brown   red
[ ]

[ ]

orange   yellow   blue   purple   green
[ ]

yellow   green   purple   purple   purple   green
[ ]

Read and Understand Grade K EMC 637

Making a Pattern

Color the beads. Finish the pattern.

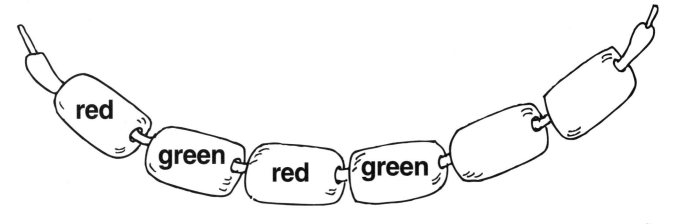

red   green   red   green

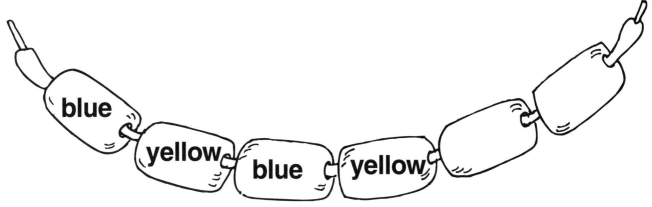

blue   yellow   blue   yellow

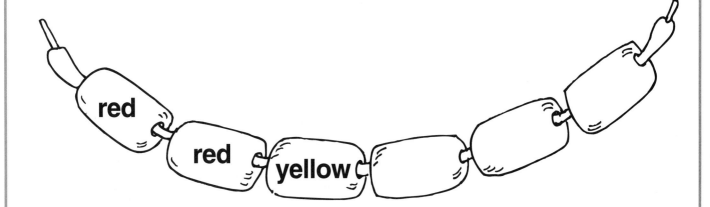

red   red   yellow

Name _____

Words That Rhyme

Circle the pictures in each line that rhyme.

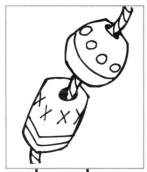
beads

seeds

bed

bugs

can

man

cat

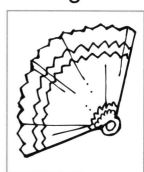
fan

bed

thread

bread

bear

one

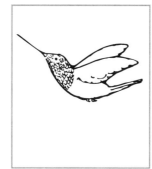
bird

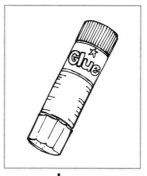
glue

shoe

Read and Understand Grade K EMC 637

The Ball Game

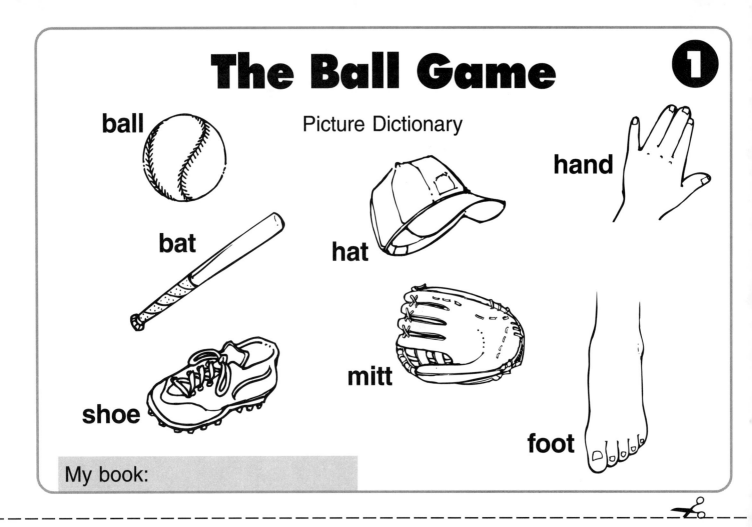

ball

bat

shoe

Picture Dictionary

hat

mitt

hand

foot

My book:

one head, one hat
one hand, one mitt

EMC 637

one foot, one shoe
one ball, one bat

one swing, one hit
one run for you

EMC 637

©1997 by Evan-Moor Corp.

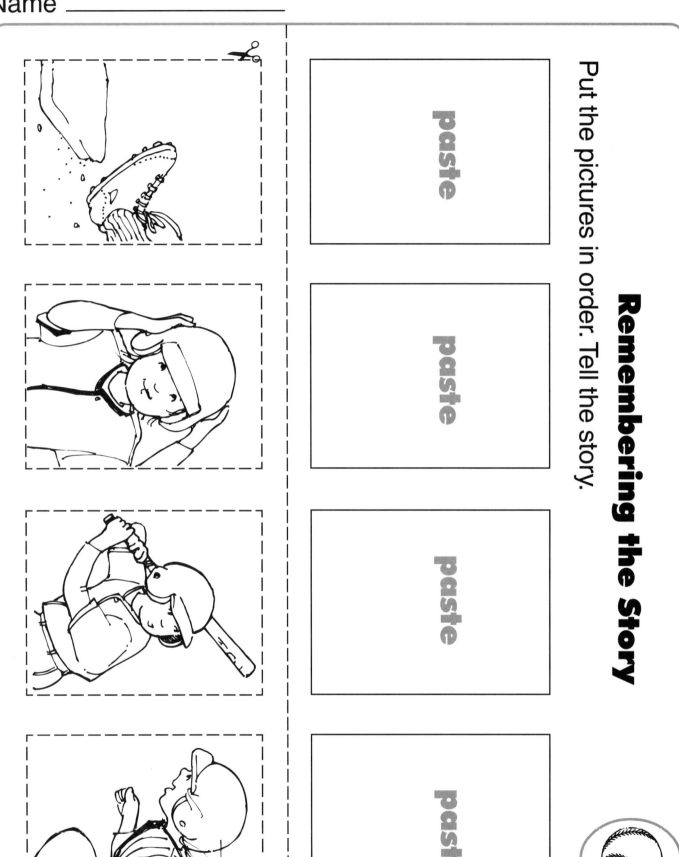

Remembering the Story

Put the pictures in order. Tell the story.

paste

paste

paste

paste

Same Sound

Color the pictures that begin with the same sound as  mitt .

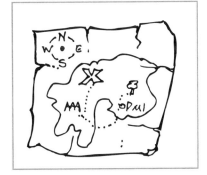

What Do You Need?

Cut and paste to show the things that you need.

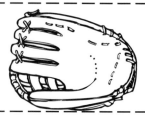

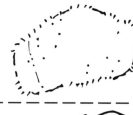

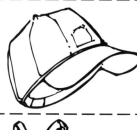

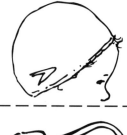

Things for Ball Game

Things for Swimming

Read and Understand Grade K EMC 637

Name _____

Make a Little Book

Draw to finish the book.

✂

The Ball Game

by _____

a ball

a bat

a mitt

a hat

Come play a game.

Read and Understand Grade K EMC 637

Swim, Swim

Picture Dictionary

fish

My book:

Swim, swim, Little Fish.
Swim fast.

Swim slow.

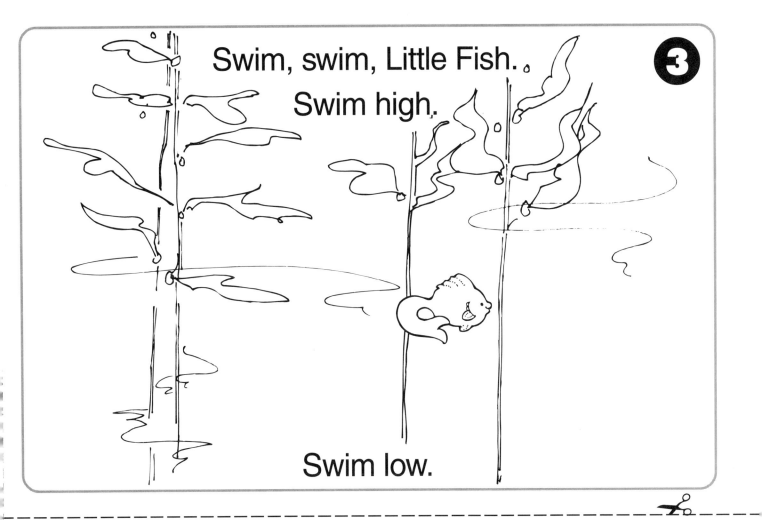

Swim, swim, Little Fish.
Swim high.

Swim low.

EMC 637

Swim, swim, Little Fish.
I have to go.

Remembering the Story

Color and cut out the fish. Tape it to a straw.
Use the fish puppet to retell the story.

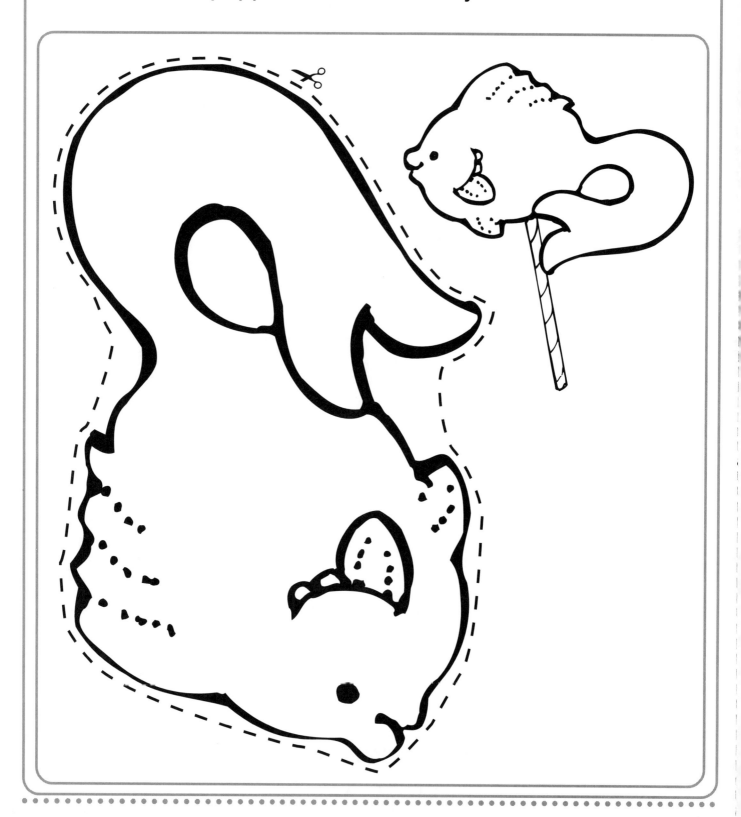

Read and Understand Grade K EMC 637

Opposites

Color, cut, and paste to show the opposites.

paste	paste
something fast	**something slow**
paste	paste
something high	**something low**

Name _____

Reading Colors

Color the fish.

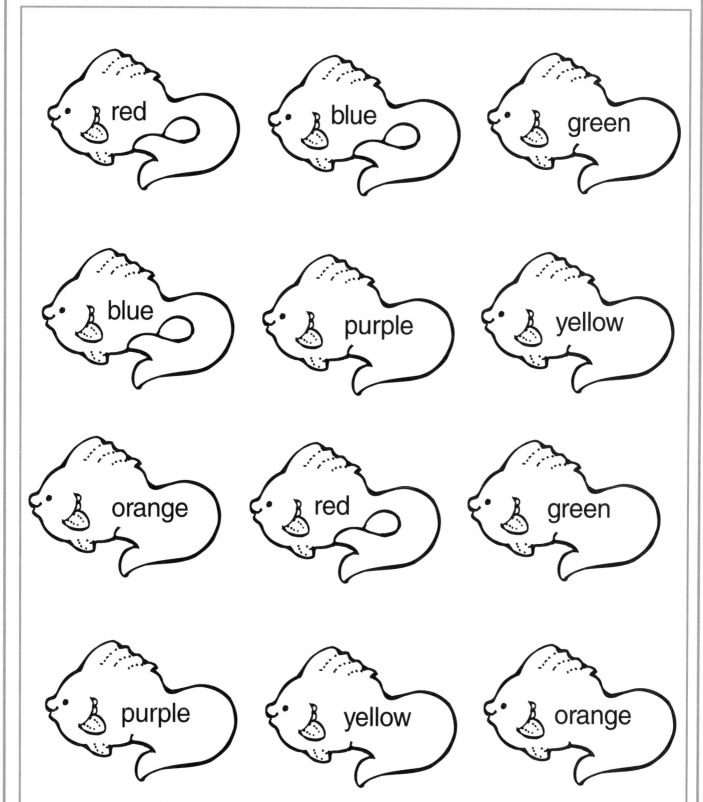

red

blue

green

blue

purple

yellow

orange

red

green

purple

yellow

orange

Read and Understand Grade K EMC 637

Name _____

Big or Little?

Cut and paste.

What is big?	What is little?

Stop and Go

sun   Picture Dictionary   top

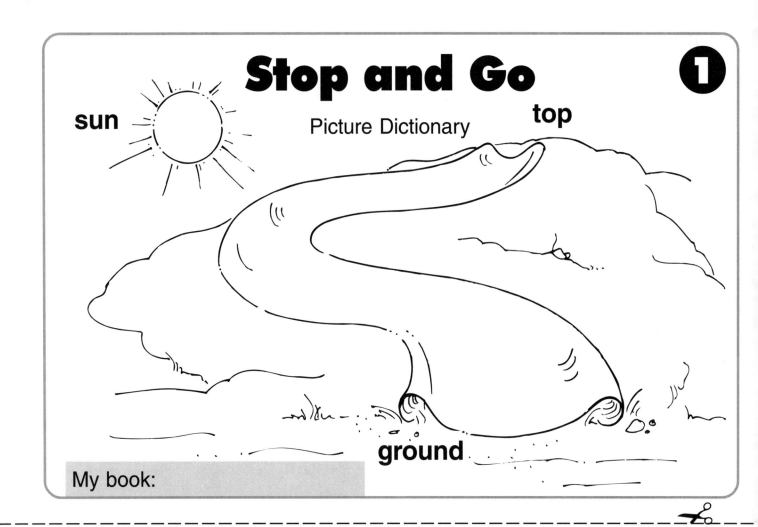

ground

My book:

2

EMC 637

We stop and go.
We go and stop.
Now here we are
Up on the top.

106

©1997 by Evan-Moor Corp.

3

We go around
And round and round
Until we're here
Safe on the ground.

4

Come play with me.
Let's have some fun
Stopping and going
In the sun.

EMC 637

Name _____

Remembering the Story

Put the pictures in story order.

Tell the story.

paste	paste	paste

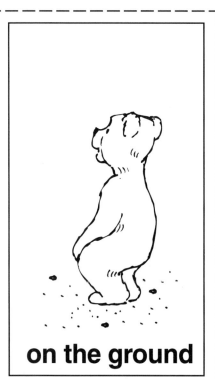

on the ground

on the top

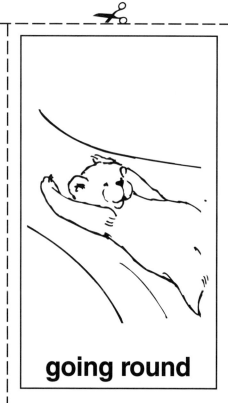

going round

Same Sound

Cut and paste to show the pictures
that begin with the sound that T stands for.

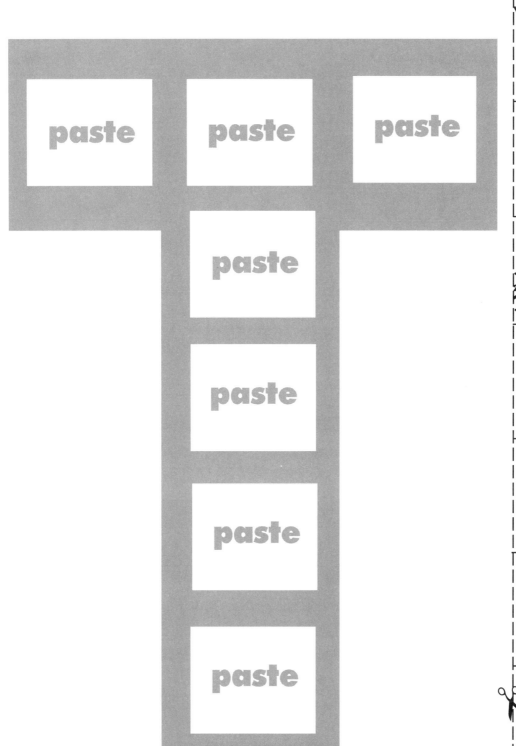

Name _____

Stop and Go

Cut and paste to show stop and go.

Stop

paste	paste	paste

Go

paste	paste	paste

Fun in the Sun

Draw four ways you have fun in the sun.

Tell about the pictures.

Trucks

Picture Dictionary

trucks

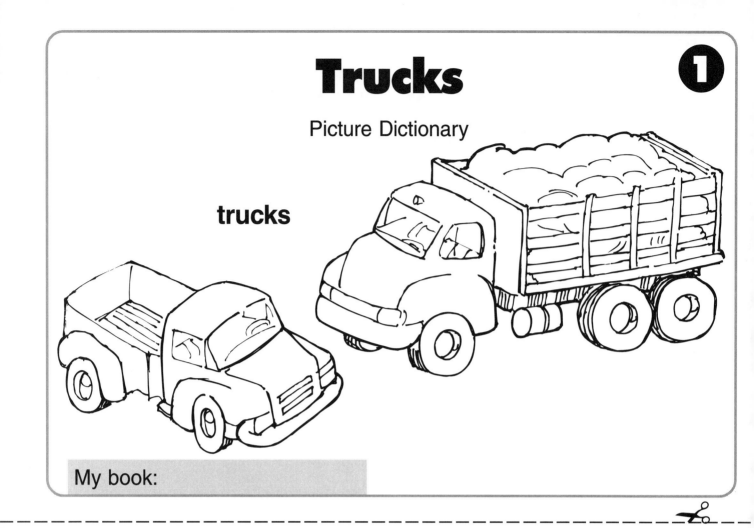

My book:

✂

EMC 637

I like trucks.

I like big trucks.

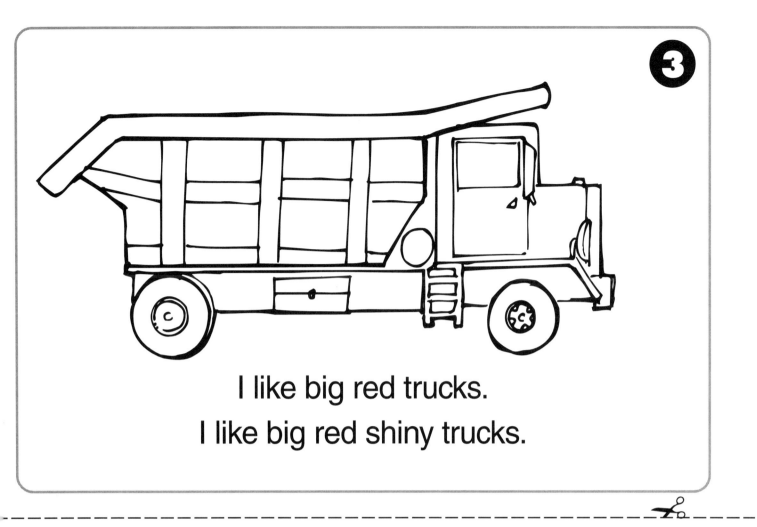

I like big red trucks.

I like big red shiny trucks.

EMC 637

I like big red shiny fire trucks.

Remembering the Story

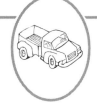

Draw to answer the questions.

What does the storyteller like?

What color is the firetruck?

Where will the firetruck go?

Name _____

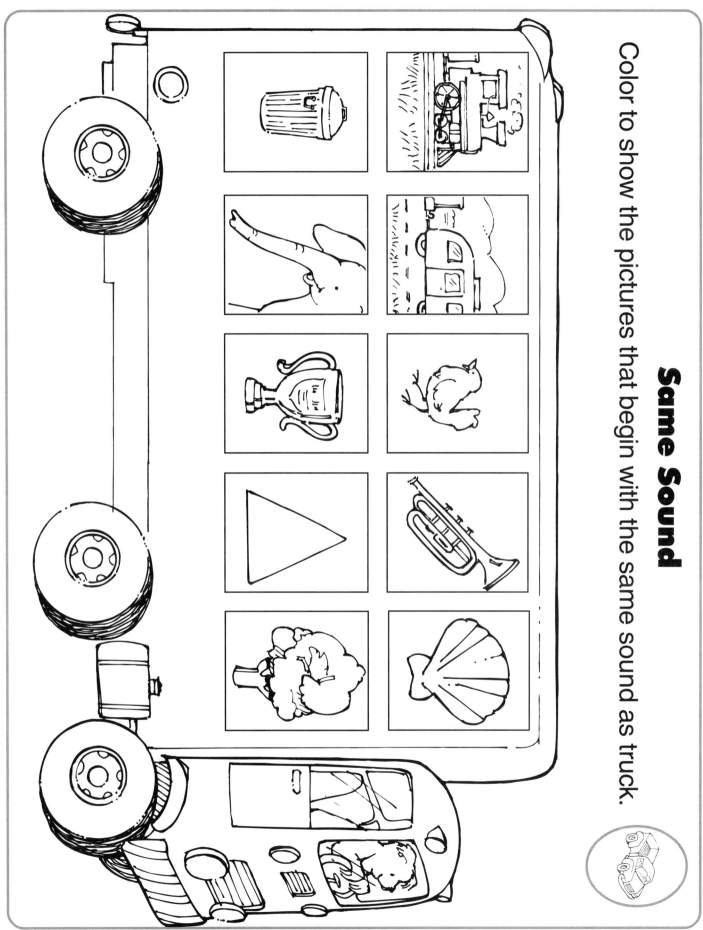

Same Sound

Color to show the pictures that begin with the same sound as truck.

Read and Understand Grade K EMC 637

Name _____

Put the Trucks Together

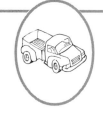

Cut the pieces, put them together, and paste them to another piece of paper.

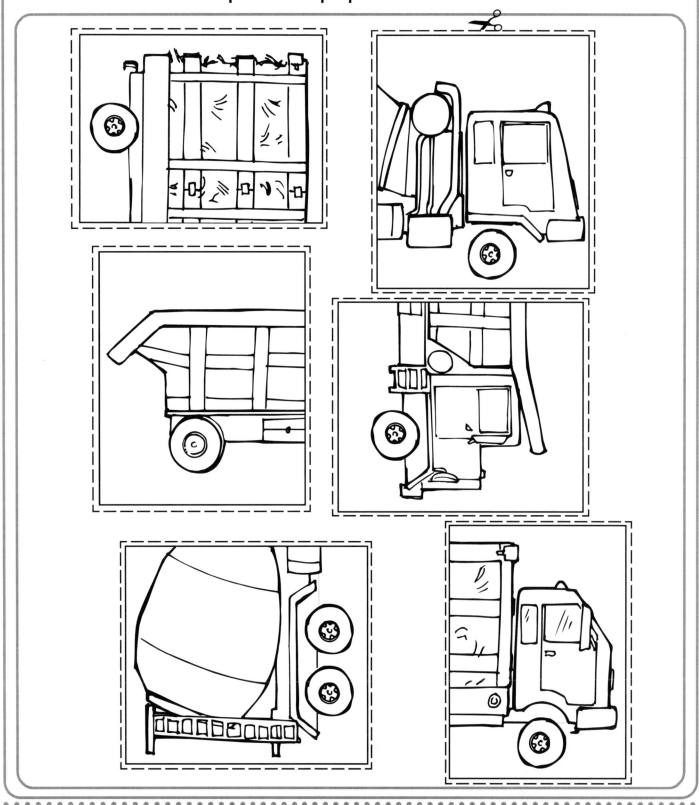

Read and Understand Grade K EMC 637

Name _____

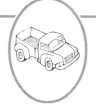

I Like...

Draw and write to show four things that you like.

I like...	I like...
I like...	I like...

Read and Understand Grade K EMC 637

The Parade

Picture Dictionary

bird

dog

cat

mouse

My book:

EMC 637

Come with me, Dog.

Come with me, Cat.

Come with me, Little Bird.
Come with me, Mouse.

EMC 637

Come with me and join the parade.

Name _____

The Parade

Cut and paste to show what each word means.

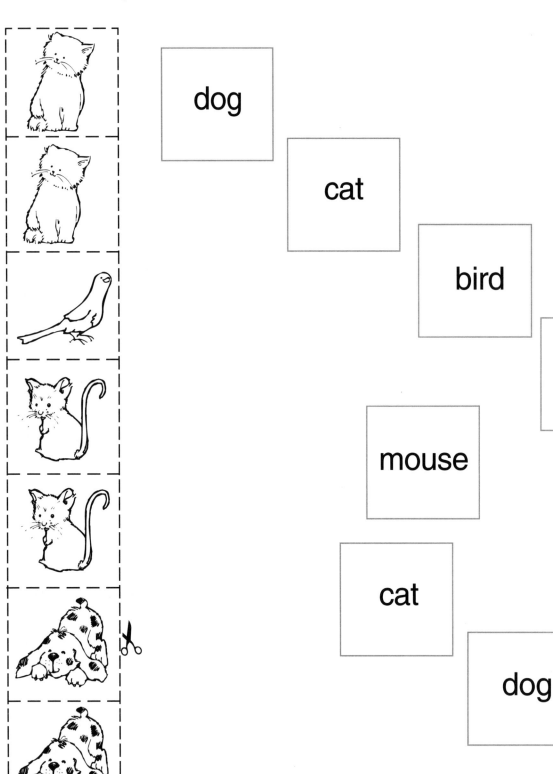

dog

cat

bird

mouse

mouse

cat

dog

The at Family

Write the words.

c + at	---------------------------------
b + at	---------------------------------
m + at	---------------------------------
r + at	---------------------------------
f + at	---------------------------------

Draw a cat with a bat.	Draw a fat rat.

  Read and Understand Grade K EMC 637

Name _____

Match the Shapes

Cut and paste to match the shapes on the flags.

Name _____

Seeing Words

Circle the words in each row that are the same as the first word.

come	come	come	cat	come

me	mom	me	me	mat

with	with	will	with	with

and	ant	and	and	and

the	the	the	to	the

Cut and paste. Build a sentence.

paste	paste	paste

with	me.	Come

Where Are the Pups?

Picture Dictionary

barn

yard

pen

house

My book:

One pup...in the yard.
Two pups...in the car.

EMC 637

Three pups...in the house.

Four pups...in the barn.

3

Five pups...in the pen.

Six pups...in a heap.

4

EMC 637

Remembering the Story

Cut and paste. Tell how many.

pups in the car

paste

pups in the barn

paste

pups in the pen

paste

pups in the yard

paste

pups in the house

paste

pups in a heap

paste

| 1 | 2 | 3 | 4 | 5 | 6 |

Same Sound

Color the pictures to show the words that begin with the sound that P stands for.

Name _____

S at the End

Draw to show how the **s** at the end changes the word.

pup	pups
car	cars
house	houses

Read and Understand Grade K EMC 637

Name _____

In the Jar

Draw in the jar.

Make: one blue .

two green .

three brown .

four black .

Read and Understand Grade K EMC 637

Name _____

Where Are They?

Write to tell where the different animals are.

Where is the bird? _____

Where are the ducks? _____

Where are the cats? _____

Where are the fish? _____

Words you need:

in the pond   in the grass

in the wagon   in the tree

130

In the Car

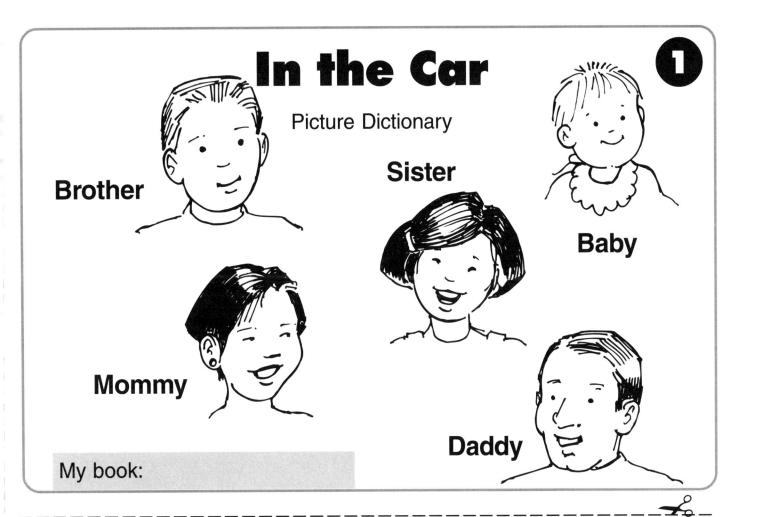

Picture Dictionary

Brother

Sister

Baby

Mommy

Daddy

My book:

Mommy drives.

Daddy sings.

EMC 637

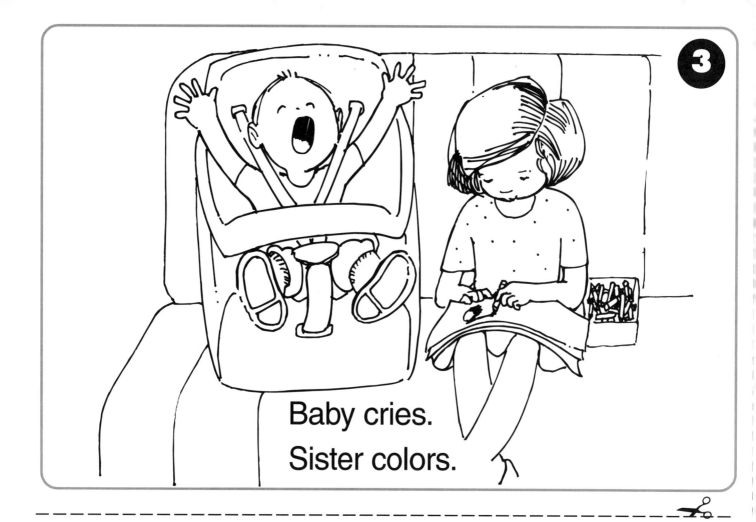

Baby cries.
Sister colors.

Brother reads
And I sleep.

EMC 637

Name _____

Remembering the Story

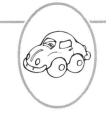

Cut and paste to tell what they did.

Mommy

| paste |

Daddy

| paste |

Baby

| paste |

Sister

| paste |

Brother

| paste |

| drives | cries | colors | sings | reads |

Name _____

Noisy or Quiet

Sort the pictures into two piles.

Make one pile a noisy pile and one pile a quiet pile.

Tell about your piles.

Read and Understand Grade K EMC 637

Name _____

The *ing* Family

Write the words. Cut and paste to show what
each word means.

s + ing	_ _ _ _ _ _ _ _ _ _ _ _ _ _ _ _ _ _	**paste**

w + ing	_ _ _ _ _ _ _ _ _ _ _ _ _ _ _ _ _ _	**paste**

r + ing	_ _ _ _ _ _ _ _ _ _ _ _ _ _ _ _ _ _	**paste**

k + ing	_ _ _ _ _ _ _ _ _ _ _ _ _ _ _ _ _ _	**paste**

Read and Understand Grade K EMC 637

Name _____

When Would You...

Cut and paste.

Night

Day

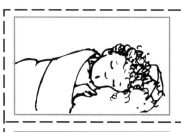 sleep

 read

 play

 run

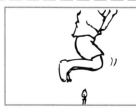 jump

 ride

Read and Understand Grade K EMC 637

My Family

Draw your family.
Tell who each person is.

Growing Up

Picture Dictionary

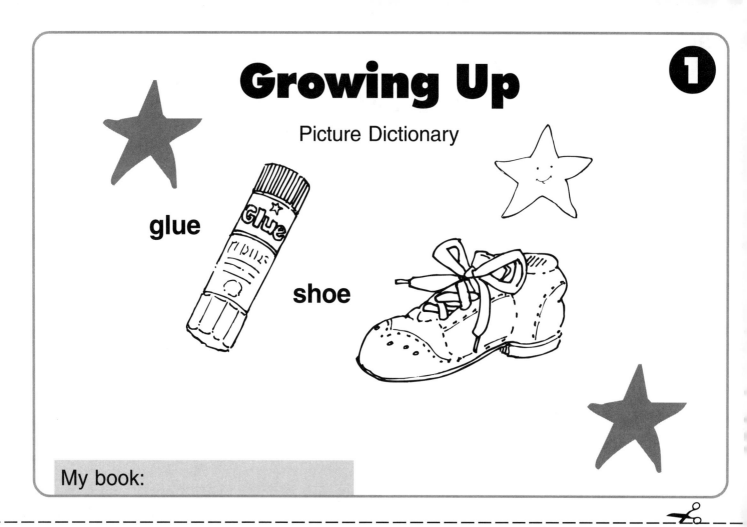

glue

shoe

My book:

EMC 637

I'm growing up.

I can use the glue.

I'm growing up. **3**

I can tie my shoe.

I'm growing up. **4**

I can read to you.

EMC 637

Remembering the Story

Draw to show the three things in the story that the kindergartner can do.

1.

2.

3.

Name _____

A New Page

Write and draw to make a new page for *Growing Up*.

✂ -

I'm growing up.
I can_____.

5

✂ -

Growing Up

Put the pictures in order to show growing up.

paste

paste

paste

paste

Words That Rhyme

Circle the two pictures in each row that rhyme.

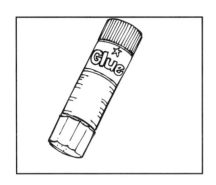  

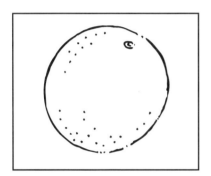  

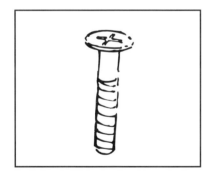  

Name _____

How Are They Alike?

Draw and write to tell how they are alike.